NICOLE W

HE STUDY OF

joseph

OUND FAITHFUL WHEN LIFE IS LESS THAN

First Edition: 2019
The Study of Joseph/Nicole Wiencek
Paperback ISBN: 978-1-946453-89-1
eBook ISBN: 978-1-946453-90-7

EQUIP PRESS

Colorado Springs

CONTENT

TO ACCESS THE VIDEO MESSAGES THAT GO ALONG WITH THIS STUDY, OPEN THE CAMERA ON YOUR PHONE AND PLACE OVER THE QR CODE.

YOU CAN ALSO TYPE IN THIS LINK ON YOUR COMPUTER!
HTTP://TINY.CC/UUDH9Y

VIDEOS EDITED BY MIKE HOLLOWAY

Endorsements

NICOLE IS CREATIVE, FUNNY, INVITING AND SPIRIT LED AS SHE NAVIGATES THE LIFE OF JOSEPH AND THE IMPACT HIS LIFE CAN HAVE ON OURS. YOU WILL LAUGH, YOU WILL CRY, AND YOU WILL EXPERIENCE GOD AT WORK IN YOUR LIFE ON A WHOLE NEW LEVEL. IF YOU ARE A WOMAN LOOKING TO BEGIN OR DEEPEN A RELATIONSHIP WITH GOD, YOU WILL NOT BE DISAPPOINTED!

-JESSICA THOMPSON, NATIONAL VICE PRESIDENT,
ARBONNE INTERNATIONAL

THIS IS AN INSIGHTFUL, RELEVANT BIBLE STUDY. NICOLE HAS GLEANED FROM AN ANCIENT STORY AND USED IT TO ASSIST YOUR CURRENT SITUATION IN A VERY PERSONAL WAY. HER TRANSPARENCY WILL ALLOW YOU TO RELAX AND GET THE MOST OUT OF THE STUDY WITHOUT FEELINGS OF INADEQUACY OR SHAME. THE USE OF WORSHIP SONGS IN ADDITION TO THE SUPPORTING SCRIPTURES ALLOWS FOR TIME SPENT IN INTIMATE FELLOWSHIP WITH GOD AS HE TRANSFORMS & CONFORMS YOU TO THE IMAGE OF CHRIST. I RECOMMEND THIS STUDY FOR EVERYONE, NO MATTER WHERE YOU ARE IN YOUR WALK WITH THE LORD!

—SALLY SMALE, ESTABLISHING WORD MIN. &
LIFE-ON-PURPOSE-ON-HSBNTV

MANY SPEAKERS HAVE GOOD CONTENT. SOME POSSESS THE ABILITY TO CAPTIVATE AN AUDIENCE, BUT FEW CAN DO BOTH. NICOLE'S RELATIONAL STYLE IS ENGAGING, EASY TO LISTEN TO AND IN-TOUCH WITH THE TIMES. HER MESSAGE IS COMPELLING, TRANSFORMATIVE AND ROOTED IN GOD'S TIMELESS WORD.

—MICAH & AUDREY MCELVEEN,
CEO & FOUNDER, VAPOR MINISTRIES

"HOW DO WE CONTINUE TO WALK FAITHFULLY WITH GOD WHEN EVERYTHING IN OUR LIVES SEEMS TO BE FALLING APART? AREN'T WE SUPPOSED TO BE REWARDED FOR WALKING IN OBEDIENCE? ISN'T IT SUPPOSED TO BE BETTER THAN THIS?
NICOLE ADDRESSES TOUGH QUESTIONS LIKE THESE & UNWRAPS THE LIFE OF JOSEPH AND HIS DEEP FAITH IN GOD. SHE SHARES STORIES FROM HER OWN JOURNEY IN GOD WHICH WILL ENCOURAGE & HELP PREPARE YOUR HEART FOR YOUR OWN DAYS OF FIERY TRIALS. THE STUDY ENCOURAGES US TO TAKE OUR EYES OFF OF THE CIRCUMSTANCES AND LIFT THEM IN PRAYER, WORSHIP & ON GOD'S WORD TO SEE HIS TRUTH & KNOW HIS GREAT LOVE FOR US."

—BETH MILLS, PASTORAL DIRECTOR OF CONFERENCES
& RETREATS, AERONOVA

Sister in Christ,

I HAD NO PLANS OR AGENDA TO WRITE & TEACH THIS STUDY. IN FACT, I OFTEN HAD NO CLUE WHAT TO DO NEXT AND PROBABLY DID IT ALL BACKWARDS! I'VE ALWAYS BEEN DRAWN TO THE STORY OF JOSEPH... SOMETHING ABOUT IT CAPTIVATED ME. OVER THE LAST COUPLE YEARS IT WAS CONSTANTLY ON MY HEART. I WAS IN A DESPERATE TIME IN MY PERSONAL LIFE & REALLY NEEDED A WORD FROM THE LORD. SO, I DECIDED TO LOOK A LITTLE DEEPER & ASKED GOD TO REVEAL THINGS TO ME I'D NEVER SEEN BEFORE. I DIDN'T ANTICIPATE HOW MUCH IT WOULD CHANGE ME! GUYS... IT CHANGED EVERYTHING.

AS GOD BEGAN TO SHOW ME UNBELIEVABLE LESSONS FROM THIS MAN'S LIFE, I KNEW IT WAS TOO GOOD NOT TO SHARE! I BELIEVE THERE IS SOMETHING TRULY LIFE-ALTERING IF WE WILL TAKE THE TIME TO QUIET OUR HEARTS, SUBMIT OUR SPIRITS, & LISTEN TO GOD'S VOICE.

I'M PRAYING FOR YOU AS YOU STEP INTO THIS CHALLENGE. I AM SO SORRY IF YOU FIND YOUSELF IN A BROKEN OR DISAPPOINTED PLACE IN LIFE. IT'S TOUGH TO LIVE ON MISSION FOR JESUS DAILY... & EVEN HARDER WHEN WE HAVE INSECURITIES AND REJECTION TO DEAL WITH. MAY THIS BRING YOU HOPE.

JUST KNOW THAT YOU ARE SEEN. YOU ARE LOVED. YOU ARE NOT ALONE. HE'S GONNA COME THROUGH. THERE IS MORE WAITING. DON'T GIVE UP. VICTORY IS JUST ON THE OTHER SIDE.

- nicole

About the Author

A DOWN TO EARTH WOMAN WHO BELIEVES LIFE IS SHORT, JESUS IS THE ONLY ANSWER & SOMETIMES WE NEED TO REMEMBER WE HAVE A LOT TO BE THANKFUL FOR. LIKE STEAK. AND FRIENDS. AND SUNSHINE.

SHE IS DEVOTED TO PROTECTING THE TRUTH OF GOD'S WORD WHILE DELIVERING IT RELEVANTLY TO OUR CULTURE. HER 'EASY TO RELATE TO' MESSAGES WILL CHALLENGE & INSPIRE YOU. SHE HOPES YOU WILL FIND & FULFILL GOD'S PLAN FOR YOUR LIFE & BE AWAKENED TO THE URGENCY OF SALVATION ONCE AGAIN.

NICOLE & HER HUSBAND MIKE & THEIR 3 KIDS ARE LEADING A CHURCH PLANT. "THE BRIDGE FELLOWSHIP" IN COLORADO SPRINGS, CO. **TO FIND OUT MORE: GO TO WWW.NICOLEWIENCEK.COM**

Designed by Maegan Hennessy

WHAT MAKES THIS STUDY DIFFERENT ————— FROM OTHERS?

INTRODUCING A NEW WAY TO DO BIBLE STUDY-VISUAL, INTERACTIVE AND REVOLUTIONARY. THIS FORMAT IS CENTERED AROUND FAITH-IN-ACTION.

THIS IS FOR YOUR MODERN DAY WOMAN. FOR THE WORKING OR STAY AT HOME MOMS, BUSY GRANDMOTHERS, MINISTRY LEADERS AND CEO'S.

FOR EVERY WOMAN WHO FEELS LIKE THERE'S JUST NOT ENOUGH TIME IN THE DAY, BUT DOESN'T WANT TO SETTLE IN HER PURSUIT OF CHRIST.

GODS WORD IS MORE POWERFUL THAN MINE COULD EVER BE. THE FAITH-IN-ACTION CONCEPT IS DESIGNED TO EQUIP GOD'S PEOPLE WITH HOW TO GET BACK INTO HIS WORD AGAIN AND ENGAGE HEARTS IN A RELEVANT WAY. I PRAY YOU WILL RELATE TO THE REAL LIFE STRUGGLES AND ULTIMATELY. . . BE INSPIRED TO LIFE CHANGING ACTION.

Explanation of your
WEEKLY TIME WITH GOD

THE ONLY WAY WE CAN TRULY GROW IS TO MAKE
SPACE. WE HAVE TIME, THE QUESTION IS HOW WILL
WE USE IT? DURING THIS STUDY, I WANTED TO GIVE RELEVANT
WAYS WE CAN DEVELOP OUR FAITH &
CREATE OPPORTUNITY TO PUT THAT INTO ACTION.

EACH WEEK WILL FOCUS ON FIVE AREAS FOR
SPIRITUAL DEVELOPMENT.

FEEL FREE TO SEEK THE LORD THROUGH THE
SCRIPTURES GIVEN AT YOUR OWN PACE AND
WRITE DOWN YOUR THOUGHTS AND EXPERIENCES.

THE NEXT FEW PAGES WILL EXPLAIN HOW TO GET
THE MOST IMPACT FROM THIS STUDY.

worship

SOME OF MY FAVORITE SONGS TO LISTEN TO THAT RELATE TO THE MESSAGES EACH WEEK. MUSIC SPEAKS TO US IN WAYS THAT CAN LIFT OUR SPIRITS AND RENEW OUR MINDS. SO TURN UP THE VOLUME, SET YOUR PLAYLIST & MAKE A JOYFUL NOISE!

praise

IT'S ALL ABOUT PERSPECTIVE. THE BOOK OF PSALMS WILL HELP US DECLARE HOW GOOD GOD IS. IF WE CHOOSE TO GIVE HIM PRAISE NO MATTER WHAT WE'RE GOING THROUGH, OUR OUTLOOK ON LIFE WILL CHANGE. REMEMBER HE IS THE SAME WORTHY GOD ON OUR BEST DAYS AND OUR WORST. EACH WEEK WE'LL HAVE THE OPPORTUNITY TO WRITE OUT PRAISES TO GOD IN OUR OWN WORDS. I CAN'T HELP BUT THINK OF HOW MUCH THIS WILL TOUCH THE FATHERS HEART!

Wisdom

IN EVERY STAGE OF LIFE WE NEED WISDOM. GOT CHILDREN?
DIFFICULT PEOPLE IN YOUR LIFE? UMMM. . .MARRIED? READING
PROVERBS WILL REMIND US THAT "WE DON'T KNOW IT ALL "
AND SHOW US HOW WE CAN FIND HIS PATH FOR OUR LIVES,
BY SEEKING HIM FOR DIRECTION. JAMES 1:5 - "IF ANYONE
LACKS WISDOM, HE SHOULD ASK GOD, WHO GIVES GENEROUSLY
WITHOUT FINDING FAULT, AND IT WILL BE GIVEN TO HIM."

Growth

THESE WEEKLY PASSAGES OF SCRIPTURE ARE DESIGNED TO
CHALLENGE US IN OUR FAITH AND HELP US TAKE OUR NEXT
STEP IN FOLLOWING JESUS. IT'S OK IF SOME OF THESE VERSES
ARE HARD TO HEAR. EMBRACE CONVICTION. IT ALLOWS GOD TO
REFINE AND SHAPE US INTO WHO HE'S CALLING US TO BE.

weekly time with **GOD**

faith in Action

WE "DO CHURCH" AND BIBLE STUDIES LEARNING ABOUT JESUS
. . .BUT WHAT ARE WE DOING WITH IT? THE BIBLE SAYS FAITH
WITHOUT WORKS IS DEAD. (JAMES 2:17) I DON'T KNOW ABOUT
YOU, BUT I WANT TO BE A WOMAN WHO IS ALIVE FOR CHRIST.

CAN WE BE HONEST WITH OURSELVES? LET'S DECIDE IF WE ARE
GOING TO BE "HEARERS" OF THE WORD. . .OR "DOERS". (JAMES
1:22) I DON'T WANT TO JUST ATTEND ANYMORE. I WANT TO PUT
MY FAITH INTO ACTION AND SEE LIVES CHANGED.

THERE WILL BE WEEKLY ACTION STEPS ENCOURAGING US TO PUT
INTO PRACTICE WHAT WE'VE LEARNED. WE ARE CALLED TO GO
AND MAKE A DIFFERENCE WITH THIS SHORT LIFE - REMEMBER
---- IT'S NOT ABOUT OUR COMFORT, IT'S ALL ABOUT REACHING
OTHERS WITH THE SAVING HOPE OF JESUS!

Weekly time with GOD

ARE YOU **READY**?

WEEK 1

Insecurity & jealousy

"GOD FORBID
WE MISS THE
GOOD IN
OTHERS
BECAUSE
WE ARE
BLINDED BY
OUR OWN
INSECURITIES."

WEEK ONE *Video Guide*

GENESIS CHAPTER 37

> THIS _____ IS FOR _____.

> ALTHOUGH THIS STUDY IS FOR ME, ITS NOT JUST _____ ME.

GENESIS CHAPTER 37:2-4

> WHY DID JOSEPH'S BROTHERS HATE HIM?
_____

> IT IS POSSIBLE TO _____ ON AMAZING PEOPLE BECAUSE
WE ARE _____ BY OUR OWN _____.

> MANY TIMES ITS OUR OWN INSECURITIES THAT CAUSE US TO
_____, _____ OR
_____ OTHER PEOPLE.

> WE ALL HAVE RELATIONSHIPS WE LOOK AT THROUGH A _____
LENSE. THE QUESTION IS DO WE RECOGNIZE IT?

> JOSEPH'S BROTHERS _____ WASN'T ACTUALLY
_____.

> OUR _____ THAT WE THINK IS SO TRUE, MAY NOT
BE _____.

> WHAT INSECURITIES DO YOU BRING INTO RELATIONSHIPS?

_____

_____

_____

GALATIANS 5:19-26

> WHAT "LENSES" SHOULD WE LOOK AT PEOPLE THROUGH BASED ON THE FRUITS
OF THE SPIRIT? _____

_____

_____

> YOU ARE A _____ OF GOD AND YOU
ARE _____.

COLOSSIANS 3:12

> YOU ARE _____.

> YOU ARE _____

_____.

> THE ENTIRE STORY OF JOSEPH STARTED WITH _____
& _____.

NOTES:_____

_____

_____

_____

_____

_____

_____

_____

_____

_____

_____

_____

_____

MY MAIN TAKE AWAY

TALK IT OUT...

WEEK ONE GROUP DISCUSSION / PERSONAL REFLECTION

1. Do we recognize that some of the issues we have with people are really issues we have with ourselves?

2. What "lenses" have we been looking at people through?

3. Read Colossians 3:12. Which "spiritual lens" is the hardest for you to see people through?

4. Discuss the definition of faithfulness. (if you don't know it...try google)

5. Is there a time in your life where you've said, "I will" to God?

WEEK ONE. TIME WITH GOD.

WHATEVER GOD IS ASKING US TO DO, WHEREVER HE IS CALLING US TO GO. . .WHAT WOULD OUR LIVES LOOK LIKE IF WE STARTED EACH DAY WITH THIS THOUGHT- "GOD, IF YOU LEAD. . . I WILL."

IT'S SO SIMPLE, YET LIFE ALTERING. WE LIMIT WHAT WE THINK HE CAN DO BECAUSE WE FOCUS ON OUR OWN WEAKNESSES, INADEQUACIES OR LIMITATIONS. WHAT IF IT HAS NOTHING TO DO WITH US AND EVERYTHING TO DO WITH OBEDIENCE?

IT'S NOT ABOUT WHO WE ARE, IT'S ABOUT WHO HE IS.

EVERY TIME IN MY LIFE GOD HAS ASKED ME TO STEP OUT IN FAITH TO DO SOMETHING FOR HIS KINGDOM - HE HAS COME THROUGH. EVERY. SINGLE. TIME. CAN YOU DO SOMETHING FOR YOURSELF? RIGHT NOW, AS YOU BEGIN THIS WEEK, WILL YOU HUMBLE YOUR HEART? WHETHER YOU NEED TO PHYSICALLY BOW YOUR HEAD, LIFT YOUR HANDS IN SURRENDER OR PRAY ON YOUR KNEES TO SHOW A POSTURE OF REVERENCE, WILL YOU ASK HIM TO SHOW YOU HIS DESIRES? HIS WILL?

ASK HIM TO REFINE, FORGIVE AND ENCOURAGE YOU. TO DO A NEW WORK AND GIVE YOU COURAGE TO STEP INTO WHATEVER HE HAS FOR YOU.

AS WE HEAD INTO THIS FIRST WEEK OF OUR TIME WITH GOD, LETS LEAVE THE "WHAT IF'S" AND RESERVATIONS BEHIND. LETS STOP TRYING TO FIGURE HOW EVERYTHING IS GOING TO WORK OUT AND JUST LET GOD BE GOD AGAIN IN OUR LIVES.

ALL WE NEED TO BRING IS A WILLING HEART.

WORSHIP
HE IS LORD (ELEVATION WORSHIP)
ANOTHER HALLELUJAH (BETHEL)
IN THE HIGHEST (CITIPOINTE WORSHIP)

PRAISE
PSALMS 95 & 96
Express thoughts of praise in
your own words.

My Fave - Psalm 95:6 Why: I often get too busy and need
to be reminded to stop and humble myself before our Creator.

WISDOM
PROVERBS CHAPTERS 1-3

My Fave: Prov 3:5-6   Why: I want my children to see me depend on God. To see me seek Him for direction and trust He'll work it out even when it doesn't make sense.

> ### MY PRAYER FOR WISDOM THIS WEEK:

GROWTH
JAMES CHAPTERS 1-5

What challenged me the most from these scriptures? What am I going to do about it?

FAITH IN ACTION.

REACH OUT TO SOMEONE THIS WEEK THAT YOU NORMALLY WOULD NOT REACH OUT TO. ASK GOD FOR YOU TO SEE THEM THE WAY HE DOES & DO SOMETHING KIND FOR THEM.

WHO DID I REACH OUT TO?

WHAT HAPPENED?

HOW DO YOU FEEL?

PRAYER TIME. . .WHO CAN YOU PRAY FOR TODAY?

WEEK ONE. TIME WITH GOD.

WEEK 2

rejection & confession

"ONE PERSON
STANDING UP
FOR WHAT'S
RIGHT CAN
CHANGE THE
COURSE OF
HISTORY."

WEEK TWO *Video Guide*

> GENESIS 37:6-9

> NOT EVERYONE IS A GOOD _____ TO SHARE WHAT GOD SHOWS US.

> YOU NEED TO KNOW WHO IS _____ YOU , WHO WILL _____ YOU AND WHO WILL ONLY _____ YOU.

VS 10-11

> OTHERS MAY DOUBT, BUT IT DOES NOT MEAN IT WILL NOT _____ _____ _____.

> WHAT DREAM HAS GOD GIVEN YOU?

> DON'T LET THE JOURNEY, LIFE'S _____ OR _____ KILL THE DREAMS GOD HAS PUT ON YOUR HEART.

VS 12-20

> UNCHECKED _____ TAKES US TO _____ PLACES.

VS 21-22

> ONE PERSON _____ UP FOR _____ RIGHT CAN _____ THE COURSE OF _____.

> WHERE ARE WE _____ WHERE WE NEED TO _____ UP?

> WHERE IS GOD ASKING YOU TO _____ _____ _____ ?

VS 23-28 - JOSEPH WAS _____, _____ AND REJECTED BY HIS OWN.

LUKE 17:25, JOHN 1:11, MATT 27:27-45

HE WAS REJECTED SO WE COULD BE _____ ROM 6:23

WE HAVE A PART TO _____. OUR PART IS _____.
ROM 10:9

GEN 37: 29-35

HOW CAN WE WALK FAITHFULLY THROUGH REJECTION? BY SAYING "NOT _____ _____ BUT _____." MATT 26:39

NOTES:_____

_____

_____

_____

_____

_____

_____

_____

_____

_____

_____

_____

_____

MY MAIN TAKE AWAY

TALK IT OUT...

1. Has there been a time in your life where you have "owned your part" & confessed your need for Jesus to save you?

2. In what area in your life is God asking you to "be the one"? Who needs you to "stand in the gap" for them?

3. Which do you relate to the most---betrayal, rejection, bitterness or confession? Why?

4. How does what i've learned apply to me & what am I going to do about it?

WEEK TWO. TIME WITH GOD.

SOMETIMES WE CAN LOOK AT OUR LIVES AND START TO FEEL LIKE IT'S LESS THAN WE THOUGHT IT WOULD BE. WE THINK OF ALL THE HOPES WE ONCE HAD, THE DREAMS THAT NEVER CAME TO PASS. WE REMEMBER PEOPLE WHO LET US DOWN OR HAVEN'T SUPPORTED US ALONG THE WAY. JUST LIKE JOSEPH, YOU MAY HAVE TO ENDURE HEARTACHE AND TRIAL. . .

BUT IF GOD HAS CALLED YOU TO SOMETHING. . .HE WILL BRING YOU THROUGH. WHEN LIFE IS LESS THAN, HOLD ON TO THE PROMISES HE'S GIVEN YOU. DON'T STOP DREAMING. THIS WEEK, ASK THE LORD TO HELP SHIFT YOUR FOCUS FROM WHAT YOU NEED, TO WHAT OTHERS MAY BE NEEDING FROM YOU.

IT'S NOT A LACK OF OPTIONS. MOST OF THE TIME WE ARE TOO BUSY WITH OUR OWN SCHEDULES THAT WE MISS THE PEOPLE ALL AROUND US. WE CAN BECOME CALLOUSED AND LOOK AWAY WHEN WE SHOULD BE SPEAKING UP. HAVE WE EVER THOUGHT, MAYBE GOD IS SHOWING US A PROBLEM SO WE CAN BE A PART OF THE SOLUTION?

LIKE THE COURAGEOUS PEOPLE WE TALKED ABOUT, JUST LIKE REUBEN WHO UNKNOWINGLY SAVED HIS ENTIRE FAMILY BY STANDING UP FOR JOSEPH. . . YOU AND I CAN CHANGE HISTORY. IT MAY START WITH SOMETHING SMALL, IT MAY BEGIN IN OUR HOMES, WITH OUR KIDS, GRANDCHILDREN AND FAMILIES. STAY FAITHFUL. IT JUST MIGHT HAVE A GREATER IMPACT THAT YOU WILL EVER KNOW.

LET'S TRY TO LIVE OUT THE WORDS OF OUR SAVIOR THIS WEEK. JESUS WAS PRAYING IN THE GARDEN BEFORE GOING TO FACE HIS DEATH ON THE CROSS. EVEN THOUGH HE WAS WILLING, JESUS KNEW ALL HE WOULD HAVE TO ENDURE. . .THE PAIN, THE SUFFERING. HE ASKS GOD IF THERE IS ANY OTHER WAY, THEN HE SAYS TO THE FATHER. . ."NOT MY WILL BE DONE, BUT YOURS."

WORSHIP
HALLELUJAH HERE BELOW (ELEVATION WORSHIP)
MAN OF SORROWS (HILLSONG - GLORIOUS RUINS)
GOOD GRACE- (HILLSONG WORSHIP)

PRAISE
PSALMS 97 & 98
Express thoughts of praise in your
own words.

My Fave - Psalm 97:4. Why: Such a vivid picture of our
awesome Creator. At His power. . .the whole earth trembles.

WEEK TWO. **TIME WITH GOD.**

WISDOM
PROVERBS CHAPTERS 4-6

My Fave: Proverbs 4:23 Why: If God says "Above all else" We should take that seriously. My heart needs protecting, especially against feelings that lead me astray.

> ### MY PRAYER FOR WISDOM THIS WEEK:

GROWTH
EPHESIANS CHAPTERS 1-6

What challenged me the most from these scriptures? What am I going to do about it?

FAITH IN ACTION.

OWN YOUR PART! NO SERIOUSLY---
TAKE TIME TO APOLOGIZE TO ANYONE YOU HAVE WRONGED.

IF YOU'VE NEVER PUT YOUR FAITH IN JESUS, CALL SOMEONE & ASK THEM TO SHOW YOU HOW!
READ ROMANS 10:9 --- CONFESS & BELIEVE!

WHO DO YOU NEED TO APOLOGIZE TO?

HOW DID IT GO?

HAVE YOU EVER PUT YOUR FAITH IN JESUS? DO YOU KNOW
FOR SURE WHERE YOU WILL SPEND ETERNITY?

PRAYER TIME. . .WHO CAN YOU PRAY FOR TODAY?

WEEK TWO. TIME WITH GOD.

WEEK 3

honor in the trial

"GOD CAN
USE MANS
BETRAYAL OR
LIFE'S TRIALS
TO WORK OUT
HIS AMAZING
WILL."

WEEK THREE *Video Guide*

GENESIS 39:2-4

> EVEN WHEN WE CAN'T _____ _____ OUR GOD IS _____
_____.

> FAR TOO OFTEN _____ GETS BLAMED FOR _____
SINFUL CHOICES.

> HOW OFTEN DO WE LET _____ KEEP US FROM SEEING
THE SMALL STEPS OF VICTORY IN OUR LIFE?

> WE DO NOT HAVE TO HAVE IT ALL TOGETHER FOR GOD TO BE
_____ IN OUR LIFE.

MATTHEW 5:16, MATTHEW 5:43-47

> "_____ YOUR ENEMY & _____ FOR
THOSE WHO PERSECUTE YOU. "PHILIPPIANS 2:14-15

> MAYBE GOD WANTS TO USE OUR LIVES TO _____ BRIGHTER
IN THE DARK TIMES.

GENESIS 39: 5-9

> IS OUR _____ TO GOD BASED ON OUR
_____ ?

GENESIS 39:10-12

> SOMETIMES WE SHOULD STAND AND FIGHT, AND OTHER TIMES WE NEED TO
_____.

1 CORINTHIANS 6:18

> WHAT ARE SOME THINGS IN OUR LIFE WE HAVE NO
_____ BEING AROUND?

> ANYONE CAN _____ INTO ANY SIN AT _____
_____.

JAMES 1:14, 1 CORINTHIANS 10:13

> GODS WORD HAS _____ _____
.... SO WHY HAVE OURS?

ROMANS 12:2, JAMES 1:27, PHILIPPIANS 4:8

> WHATEVER WE ARE PUTTING IN OUR LIVES, IS IT _____ US?
OR IS IT _____ OUR MINDS

NOTES:_____

_____

_____

_____

_____

_____

_____

_____

_____

_____

_____

_____

_____

_____

MY MAIN TAKE AWAY

TALK IT OUT...

WEEK THREE GROUP DISCUSSION / PERSONAL REFLECTION

1. Are you having a hard time seeing the good in life right now?

2. Briefly share a time when God was faithful through a trial in your life.

3. If we want victory in our life, it starts by being honest about our struggles. We all are TEMPTED. Be brave---share with the group where you are most tempted.

4. Is there an area in your life right now that you need to RUN from?

WEEK THREE. TIME WITH GOD.

WE WANT THE BLESSING OF GOD IN OUR LIVES RIGHT? I MEAN WOULD ANYONE SAY NO TO THAT? YET OFTEN WE LOOK AT AREAS WHERE OTHER PEOPLE (SPOUSE, BOSS, GROWN CHILDREN) ARE NOT FOLLOWING GOD & IT FEELS LIKE THEY ARE LIMITING THINGS FOR US.

I HAVE SOME GOOD NEWS FOR YOU! THROUGH YOUR FAITHFULNESS, THE BLESSING AND FAVOR OF GOD CAN BE ON YOUR LIFE. . . YOUR FAMILY, WORK AND MINISTRY EVEN IF EVERYONE AROUND YOU DOESN'T SEEM TO CARE. JOSEPH WAS A SERVANT IN A PAGAN HOUSEHOLD AND YET, GOD BLESSED EVERYTHING HE DID! THIS IS AMAZING! ITS SHOWS US THAT IN SPITE OF OUR CIRCUMSTANCES WE JUST NEED TO KEEP DOING OUR PART, AND GOD WILL BLESS.

AS YOU MEET WITH THE LORD THIS WEEK, ASK HIM TO REVEAL AREAS IN YOUR LIFE WHERE MAYBE YOU DON'T EVEN NOTICE. . . BUT YOU'RE STARTING TO COMPROMISE. THE LITTLE, SEEMINGLY SMALL STEPS THAT LEAD US AWAY FROM PURITY OF HEART AND MIND. A RASH WORD TEARING SOMEONE ELSE APART. . . A STOLEN GLANCE IN ANOTHER'S DIRECTION. . . A LITTLE LIE THAT DOESN'T REALLY MATTER ANYWAYS. THOUGHTS OF SELF IMPORTANCE OR PRIDE SNEAKING IN, WANTING TO ELEVATE OUR DESIRES OVER GOD'S DESIGN.

DO WE REALIZE WE ARE BEING POLLUTED DAILY? TV, MOVIES, DRAMA, MUSIC . . . THERE ARE SO MANY INFLUENCES FIGHTING TO DESTROY OUR MINDS. HAVE WE ACCEPTED CULTURE'S VIEW OF PURITY? OUR KIDS, HUSBANDS, FRIENDSHIPS, & TESTIMONY, THEY ALL ARE AT STAKE.

"ABOVE ALL ELSE GUARD YOUR HEART FOR EVERYTHING YOU DO FLOWS FROM IT." – PROVERBS 4:23

IF GOD SAYS, "ABOVE ALL ELSE" - WE SHOULD PROBABLY TAKE THIS SERIOUSLY. WHAT AREAS OF YOUR LIFE HAVE YOU "LET DOWN YOUR GUARD?"

THIS WEEK IN THE NAME OF JESUS, QUIET THOSE NEGATIVE VOICES & REMEMBER, IT'S IN THE DARKEST OF TIMES HIS LIGHT SHINES THE BRIGHTEST.

WORSHIP

NOTHING ELSE (CODY CARNES)
NONE (ELEVATION WORSHIP)
ALWAYS WORTHY (MAEGAN HENNESSY)

PRAISE

PSALMS 99 & 100

Express thoughts of praise in your own words.

My Fave - Psalm 100:4 - Our attitudes as we come into God's house of worship is so important. Whatever is going on this reminds me to come before Him with thankful heart.

WISDOM
PROVERBS CHAPTERS 7-9

My Fave - Proverbs 9:9 - Even if it's not easy to hear, I hope I never get to the place where I stop listening to wise counsel. A teachable heart can improve every area of our lives.

MY PRAYER FOR WISDOM THIS WEEK:

GROWTH
GALATIANS CHAPTERS 1-6

What challenged me the most from these scriptures? What am I going to do about it?

FAITH IN ACTION.

NO BAD VIBES. MAKE NO ROOM FOR NEGATIVITY. INSTEAD OF TALKING ABOUT ALL THE THINGS GOING WRONG. . .SHARE WITH SOMEONE EVERY DAY THIS WEEK SOMETHING GOOD GOD HAS DONE IN YOUR LIFE. RIGHT THEN AND THERE, ASK THEM HOW YOU CAN BE THERE FOR THEM & TAKE A MOMENT TO PRAY WITH THEM.

WHO DID YOU SHARE WITH & WHAT WAS THEIR RESPONSE?

HOW DID YOU FEEL AFTER PRAYING FOR SOMEONE?

PRAYER TIME. . .WHO CAN YOU PRAY FOR TODAY?

WEEK THREE. **TIME WITH GOD.**

WEEK 4

forgotten

"WHEN LIFE
GOES FROM
BAD TO
WORSE, WILL
YOU STILL
BRING HIM
GLORY?"

WEEK FOUR *Video Guide*

GENESIS 39:13-23

> GOD CAN USE THE _____ IN OUR LIFE TO PREPARE US FOR WHAT HE HAS FOR US.

> VS 21- "THE LORD WAS _____ _____.

> SOMETIMES WHEN GOD MOVES IT'S _____ AT FIRST.

> ITS SMALL STEPS OF _____ TODAY, THAT LEAD TO BIG STORIES OF _____ FOR OUR FUTURE.

GENESIS 40:1-8

> VS15- JOSEPH DIDN'T LET WHAT _____ TO HIM _____ HIM.

> VS 23- THE CUPBEARER _____ HIM.

> WE SHOULD NEVER BE SO _____ ON OURSELVES THAT WE FORGET OTHERS NEED OUR HELP.

GENESIS 41

> WHEN _____ _____ YEARS HAD PASSED.......

> GODS _____ ARE NOT OUR WAYS, HIS
_____ IS NOT OUR TIMING.

> JUST BECAUSE ITS TAKING TOO LONG, IT DOESN'T MEAN OUR PRAYER
_____ BEING _____.

> COULD IT BE THAT PERHAPS GOD HASN'T _____ US... RATHER WE
HAVE _____ WHO _____ IS?

> WHAT WE _____ ABOUT GOD WILL
_____ HOW WE WALK THROUGH THE JOURNEY.

NOTES:_____

MY MAIN TAKE AWAY

TALK IT OUT...
WEEK FOUR GROUP DISCUSSION / PERSONAL REFLECTION

1. When you feel a prayer is taking too long to be answered, what is your typical response?

2. Discuss how God's timing is different than ours.

3. Share a time you felt forgotten.

4. What can you do this week to bring Glory to God?

WEEK FOUR. TIME WITH GOD.

YOU'RE TRYING TO DO IT GODS WAY. YOU'RE GROWING, GIVING MORE OF YOURSELF AND LETTING GO OF A PAST THAT HELD YOU BACK. BUT EACH TIME YOU TRY AND MAKE PROGRESS TO PURSUE GOD MORE, SOMETHING GOES WRONG. AN UNEXPECTED BILL, A DISHEARTENING CALL FROM THE DOCTORS OFFICE, A CO-WORKER STABS YOU IN THE BACK. . .IT SEEMS YOU CAN'T SPEAK WITHOUT GETTING INTO AN ARGUMENT WITH YOUR SPOUSE AND WHAT IN THE WORLD ARE THE KIDS ON? DID SOMEONE GIVE THEM REDBULL?

SOMETIMES THINGS SEEM TO GO FROM BAD TO WORSE. WE LOOK AT EVERYTHING GOING WRONG AND WE CAN EASILY MISS THE FACT THAT GOD'S HAND IS STILL WORKING. BY NATURE WE WILL TRY TO TAKE CONTROL OF THE SITUATION IF GOD'S "TAKING TOO LONG."

I DON'T KNOW WHY GOD WORKS THE WAY HE DOES. NONE OF US IN THIS LIFETIME WILL BE ABLE TO FIGURE IT OUT. WHAT WE CAN DO, IS CHOOSE TO CLING TO HIS WORD. . .THAT HE IS WITH US, HE NEVER LEAVES US AND HE HAS PLAN THROUGH IT ALL.

WHEN THE DAYS TURN INTO YEARS, AND OUR PRAYERS DON'T SEEM TO BE GETTING THROUGH, IT'S EASY TO GIVE IN TO THOUGHTS THAT GOD HAS FORGOTTEN US. MAY YOUR HEART BE ENCOURAGED THIS WEEK. . .HOLD ON TO HOPE!! HIS TIMING IS NOT OUR TIMING. WE CANNOT CONTROL THE OUTCOME BUT WE CAN DECIDE THE POSTURE OF OUR HEART. WE CAN WALK HUMBLY AND HONOR GOD EVEN IN THE TRIAL. THIS WEEK, CAN I CHALLENGE YOU TO ASK THIS QUESTION----"WHEN LIFE IS LESS THAN, WILL I STILL BRING HIM GLORY?"

YOUR STORY IS NOT DONE YET. DON'T GIVE UP, GOD HAS THE FINAL WORD. LET'S GET OUR EYES OFF OF THE PROBLEMS AND FIX OUR GAZE ON THE ONLY ONE WHO CAN DO SOMETHING ABOUT IT.

WORSHIP

YOURS (ELEVATION WORSHIP)
DO IT AGAIN (ELEVATION WORSHIP)
BREAKTHROUGH (RED ROCKS WORSHIP)

PRAISE

PSALMS 101 & 102
Express thoughts of praise in
your own words.

My Fave - Psalm 102:1 & 17- He hears our cry! I can have
confidence that when I call out to my Father,
I know He answers me. He will respond!

WEEK FOUR. TIME WITH GOD.

WISDOM
PROVERBS CHAPTERS 10-12

My Fave - Proverbs 10:19, 11:22 / 12:4, 15-19 - When you read these, your gonna be like. . . "why are these your favorites? They are more like a smack in the face!" but hey, who doesn't need the occasional spiritual smack in the face?

MY PRAYER FOR WISDOM THIS WEEK:

GROWTH
1 PETER CHAPTERS 1-5

What challenged me the most from these scriptures? What am I going to do about it?

FAITH IN ACTION.

IT'S EASY TO GET CAUGHT UP IN OUR OWN STRUGGLES. THIS WEEK, INVITE YOUR FAMILY TO SEE WHAT YOU CAN DO TOGETHER TO MAKE SOMEONE ELSE'S LIFE BETTER.
LOOK AROUND & ASK GOD TO SHOW YOU ANYONE FEELING "FORGOTTEN". GOD OFTEN ALLOWS US TO GO THROUGH SOMETHING SO WE CAN MEET THE NEED IN SOMEONE ELSE'S LIFE. WHAT CAN YOU DO FOR THEM?.

WHAT DID YOU DO AS A FAMILY TO HELP SOMEONE?

HOW DID IT GO? JUST IN CASE IT DIDN'T GO HOW YOU PLANNED. . .IT WASN'T IN VAIN. IT'S NOT OUR JOB TO FORCE THE OUTCOME. IT'S OUR RESPONSIBILITY TO OBEY BY LOOKING FOR AND STEPPING INTO THE OPPORTUNITY. WE WATER. . .GOD GROWS. KEEP WATERING. ISAIAH 55:10-11

PRAYER TIME. . .WHO CAN YOU PRAY FOR TODAY?

WEEK FOUR. **TIME WITH GOD.**

WEEK 5

forgiveness

"GOD'S PLAN IS ALWAYS ABOUT RESCUING OTHERS."

WEEK FIVE *Video Guide*

PERHAPS OUR LIVES ARE NOT JUST MEANT FOR _____. . .BUT FOR SOMETHING _____.

GEN 41:49-57

THE FAMINE WAS SEVERE THROUGHOUT THE ENTIRE _____.

VS 42:1-10

WHEN GOD GIVES A PROMISE, NOTHING IN ALL THE _____ AND NO _____ CAN STOP IT FROM HAPPENING.

VS 16-24 - THE TEST

THE _____ FOR OUR SIN IS ALWAYS _____ THAN WE WILL WANT TO _____.

VS 24-38

_____ IS THE BROTHER WHO STEPS UP TO TRY AND MAKE IT RIGHT.

GEN 43:1-14

_____ IS THE SECOND BROTHER STEPPING UP TO TAKE RESPONSIBILITY.

GEN 44:9-33 - THE FINAL TEST

JUDAH SAYS, "_____ _____." FINALLY WE SEE TRUE _____ CHANGE.

GENESIS 45

WHEN WE HAVE THE CHOICE TO _____ OR GET _____, WHAT DO WE DO?

WHAT YOU MEANT FOR _____, GOD MEANT FOR _____.

OUR LIVES ARE NOT JUST _____ FOR US BUT FOR THE _____ OF OTHERS.

WE FORGIVE BECAUSE:

1. THE _____ IS GREAT.

2. WE HAVE BEEN _____ SO MUCH.

3. JESUS IS _____.

NOTES:_____

_____

_____

_____

_____

_____

_____

_____

_____

_____

_____

_____

MY MAIN TAKE AWAY

TALK IT OUT...
WEEK FIVE GROUP DISCUSSION / PERSONAL REFLECTION

1. Are there people in your life you need to truly forgive? What is holding you back?

2. What mistakes do you need to learn from. . .or what mistakes have you learned from?

3. Let's get real. . .What are you willing to go through to see the deliverance of others?

4. How does the last thought affect the way you view your current situation?

WEEK FIVE. TIME WITH GOD.

DO YOU THINK IF WE KNEW, I MEAN REALLY UNDERSTOOD HOW EVERYTHING WAS WORKING TOGETHER FOR A PURPOSE, AND THAT THE HARD THINGS WE WENT THROUGH WERE ACTUALLY GOING TO HELP CHANGE LIVES- OUR PERSPECTIVES WOULD CHANGE?

IT'S JUST THAT WHEN WE ARE IN THE MIDDLE OF THE TRIAL OR HEARTACHE, WE USUALLY BECOME CONSUMED BY THE PAIN. WHAT WE DON'T STOP TO THINK ABOUT IS THAT THERE IS ALWAYS MORE GOING ON THAN WE CAN FATHOM. IT'S ONLY NOW, AS WE LOOK BACK OVER THE STORY OF JOSEPH, THAT WE ARE ABLE TO SEE HOW EACH BETRAYAL, LOSS & DARK TURN IN THE ROAD WOULD LEAD TO ANOTHER PART OF GODS PLAN . . .HIS ULTIMATE PLAN TO SAVE PEOPLE.

SINCE THE FALL OF MAN; WHEN WE CHOSE TO GO AGAINST OUR CREATOR AND SIN ENTERED THE WORLD . . .GOD HAS ALWAYS BEEN WORKING OUT WAYS TO BRING HIS PEOPLE BACK TO HIM. THOSE AROUND US MAKE SINFUL CHOICES THAT HURT US. WE MAKE WRONG CHOICES THAT HURT OTHERS. BUT SOMEHOW HE IS TRYING TO CLOSE THE DISTANCE WITH HIS LOVE AND FORGIVENESS. HE SEES IT ALL. FROM THE BEGINNING OF TIME UNTIL THE DAY JESUS COMES BACK. HE KNOWS ETERNITY IS FOREVER AND THE "LIGHT AND MOMENTARY TROUBLES" OF THIS EARTH WILL PALE IN COMPARISON TO THE GLORY WE WILL EXPERIENCE IN HEAVEN.

YET HERE WE ARE, LIVING OUR DAILY LIVES, SO UPSET BY WHAT SOMEONE SAID OR WHAT THEY DIDN'T DO FOR US OR WHY WE DIDN'T GET THE THINGS WE WANTED. I THINK THE ENEMY WANTS TO GET US SO DISTRACTED BY ALL THE RELATIONSHIP STRUGGLES AND UNFORGIVENESS THAT WE TRULY FORGET WHAT THIS LIFE IS ALL ABOUT.

SISTER IN CHRIST- LIFE MAY BE LESS THAN YOU HOPED. I'M SORRY. . .TRULY, I AM. I PRAY VICTORY & BLESSING IS JUST AROUND THE CORNER FOR YOU. HOWEVER, WHATEVER YOUR CIRCUMSTANCE. . .YOU & I HAVE SO MUCH TO BE THANKFUL FOR. WE HAVE A GOD WHO LOVED US ENOUGH TO SEND HIS SON TO PAY FOR OUR SINS SO WE CAN SPEND ETERNITY IN HEAVEN. IF YOU HAVE THIS HOPE, IT IS ENOUGH. IT'S WITH THIS MINDSET, I PRAY YOU CAN RECEIVE ALL GOD HAS FOR YOU IN YOUR TIME WITH HIM THIS FINAL WEEK.

WORSHIP

SPIRIT LEAD ME (INFLUENCE MUSIC)
HERE IN THE PRESENCE (ELEVATION WORSHIP)
THIS WE KNOW (VERTICAL WORSHIP)

_____

PRAISE

PSALMS 103 & 104

Express thoughts of praise in
your own words.

My Fave - Psalm 103:1 So many good ones! This verse inspires
me to praise with every ounce of my soul. At the end of my
life, I pray what psalm 104:33 says, can be said of me.

WEEK FIVE. TIME WITH GOD.

59

WISDOM
PROVERBS CHAPTERS 13-15

My Fave - Proverbs 14:31- How beautiful to think that the Almighty God, King of the universe cares about the poor. He hears the cry of the destitute. How humbling.

MY PRAYER FOR WISDOM THIS WEEK:

GROWTH
MATTHEW CHAPTERS 5-7

What challenged me the most from these scriptures? What am I going to do about it? ?

FAITH IN ACTION.

IT'S TIME TO GIVE BACK. FIND ANOTHER WOMAN TO MEET WITH ON A REGULAR BASIS & ASK HER TO DO A WEEKLY BIBLE STUDY OR MEET FOR COFFEE ONCE A MONTH. EVERYONE NEEDS A MENTOR & NEEDS TO BE ONE.

IT DOESN'T MATTER IF YOU THINK YOU DON'T HAVE MUCH TO OFFER OR ENOUGH KNOWLEDGE TO GIVE. LET GOD USE YOUR STORY, YOUR WILLING HEART AND YOUR LOVE FOR OTHERS TO IMPACT A LIFE. . .THE WAY YOURS HAS BEEN.

LET GO. FORGIVE & TRUST GOD IS WORKING. RELEASE THEM & BE FREE.

WHO DO I FEEL LED TO POUR INTO OR WHO DO I NEED TO ASK TO POUR INTO ME?

I FORGIVE:

I LET GO OF:

PRAYER TIME. . .WHO CAN YOU PRAY FOR TODAY?

WEEK FIVE. **TIME WITH GOD.**

I'd like to leave you with one last challenge...

GOD HAS OFTEN PUT A THOUGHT ON MY HEART THAT HAS LITERALLY KEPT ME AWAKE AT NIGHT. I REMEMBER AFTER HAVING OUR SECOND CHILD I WOKE UP IN A PANICKED SWEAT. WHAT IF WHAT I SAY I BELIEVE, IS REALLY TRUE? WHAT IF HEAVEN AND HELL ARE ACTUALLY REAL? DO I BELIEVE THAT? I MEAN, DOES MY LIFE SHOW THAT I ACTUALLY BELIEVE THIS---THAT EVERYONE WILL SPEND ETERNITY IN ONE OF THESE TWO PLACES? IF YES, THEN EVERYTHING WOULD CHANGE.

IT WOULD CHANGE THE WAY I SPEAK TO PEOPLE, FORGIVE THEM, LOOK AT THEM AND TALK ABOUT THEM. IT WOULD CHANGE MY DAYS, SCHEDULE, THE WAY I SPEND MY TIME, HOW I RAISE UP MY CHILDREN AND THE WAY I SERVE IN THE CHURCH. MY ENTIRE PERSPECTIVE ABOUT LIFE WOULD BE MUCH MORE SIMPLE.

THE TRUTH IS...IT IS REAL. ALL OF IT. EVERY WORD OF THE LORD IS TRUE AND WILL COME TO PASS. WE GET ONE SHORT LIFE. ONE OPPORTUNITY TO REACH THOSE FAR FROM JESUS AND BRING THEM TO THE SAVING GRACE JESUS OFFERED BY DYING ON THE CROSS IN OUR PLACE.

A FRIEND RECENTLY SHARED THIS WITH ME...
"who are the people closest to you, yet furthest from God?"

WE CANNOT REACH EVERYONE, BUT WE CAN REACH SOME. THE LORD HAS PUT SPECIFIC PEOPLE AROUND US FOR A REASON. THEIR ETERNITY IS AT STAKE & HE IS CALLING US TO SHARE HIS LOVE, HOPE & TRUTH WITH THEM. ASK GOD TO SHOW YOU WHO "YOUR PEOPLE" ARE. WRITE THEIR NAMES ON THE NEXT PAGE & COMMIT TO PRAY FOR THEM. IF WE'RE INTENTIONAL, GOD WILL OPEN A DOOR FOR US TO SHARE.

WE ONLY HAVE ONE LIFE---LET'S MAKE THE MOST OF IT!

WHO ARE THE PEOPLE CLOSEST TO ME, YET FARTHEST FROM GOD

_____   _____

_____   _____

_____   _____

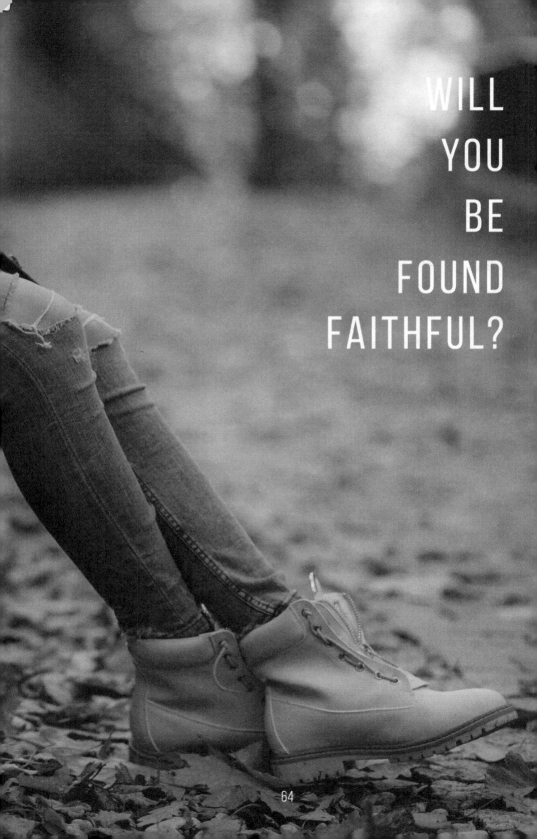

WILL
YOU
BE
FOUND
FAITHFUL?